Broug ... et
an ...

An Unofficial ...

The Pupils of S2 (2022)
Drummond Community High School.

SUPER
POWER
BOOKS

Published in 2022 by Super Power Books

Copyright Super Power Agency © 2022

S2 pupils of Drummond Community High School have asserted
the right to be identified as the authors of this Work in
accordance with the Copyright, Designs and Patents Act 1988

ISBN: 978-1-838-2568-3-8

A CIP catalogue copy of this book can be found
in the British Library.

Cover illustration by Grace Feakes
www,gracefeakes.design

Published with the help of Calum's Legacy Books
www.indieauthorsworld.com

Calum's
Legacy

Introduction

Drummond Community High School is not just a name – but a true reflection of the inner school itself and its place within the local area. After 16 (!) years of leading English, Modern Languages and our growing range of subjects within our own faculty, I often find myself reflecting on why Drummond? Why have I never felt a need for a move to work elsewhere? The answer is simple – working here is like spending every day with my extended family. Our school is very much a diverse community and last time we worked with Superpower Agency, we explored this by reflecting on what made us individuals. This time we were able to look beyond the school gates and make connections with various businesses; explore the history and see how our small locality plays a massive role within our capital city.

Thanks to the energy, imagination and dynamic team of Gerald, Sian and their volunteers our S2s were able to produce this fantastic guidebook which not only recommends and reflects on our community, but also celebrates our local area. It was a pleasure watching our young people enthuse and educate themselves over their space within their place. We hope that you find their pieces useful, enlightening and engaging and that you enjoy exploring Broughton Street and beyond.

Joanna Tindall
Curriculum Leader: Faculty of Languages & Literacy
Drummond Community High School

How to use this book

If you are in search of a typical guidebook for the area encompassing Bellevue, Broughton Street and beyond, this isn't it. It's not filled with fancy restaurants, nice but boring descriptions of what you can do on a budget, or the locations of famous people who slept or died in the buildings. If you need that book, put this one down and move on.

HOWEVER....

If you are looking for a guidebook from a young person's point of view, look no further! This book is a fun exploration of a neighbourhood brimming with shops, restaurants and new possibilities where a person around the age of 12 and up can feel comfortable. You'll learn where they hang out, where they shop and eat, and a few facts along the way. This book may be written by youth but it's for travellers of all ages looking to experience a part of the city that only residents know. We hope you enjoy it.

And I lied, there may be a nice restaurant or two in here. It is still guidebook but probably one of the most fun and creative guidebooks you'll find.

Gerald Richards
Founding CEO
Super Power Agency

Contents

Section One
History/ Then and Now

Mansfield Traquair

Jordyn R, Fiona HK, Theo T

Mansfield Traquair, often nicknamed 'Edinburgh's Sistine Chapel', is located right near Drummond High School on East London Street. Its stunning architecture makes the chapel stand out, but what lies behind those red doors and exquisite exterior and why is it so often overlooked? This chapter will be delving into the chapel's history and controversy behind the breathtaking art which lies inside.

History

Although the history around Mansfield Traquair is vague, we can still gather a pretty good idea about its past. The chapel was designed by Robert Rowan Anderson, a famous Victorian architect who was knighted in 1902. The foundation stone was laid in 1873 and was built and largely completed in 1876. In 1893, Phoebe Anna Traquair was commissioned to create a religious piece for the chapel. This was an odd thing at the time, as Phoebe was a woman and at the time women having jobs, let alone getting paid, was uncommon. This was also many years before World War I, when women had to take over jobs from men who were sent away. She was also married, which was almost unheard of. Phoebe was often inspired by romantic and renaissance art, and she was particularly known for her embroidery and similar arts. After the mural until 1958 in which a priest died ending this part of the chapel's life. It is unknown what happened in the many years that the chapel laid without purpose. But presumably it still belonged to the Catholic Church in 1974 and changed hands again to the Edinburgh Brick Company in 1988. A few years after this, the Mansfield Traquair trust was founded. And eventually bought Mansfield Traquair. In a shocking twist, Mansfield Traquair was in major disrepair after it had barely been touched since its purchase by the brick company in 1988. In the fun year of 2000, the repairs began and in the capitalist fashion show it was to incorporate offices for the Scottish Council for Voluntary Organizations. The building was given a grant by the National Lottery Heritage fund in the same year, and by 2002 the building work was complete and with the rest of the money the mural was restored.

Controversy

Currently, you can only visit the building if you book to have a wedding there. This brings up the question, should this art be free to look at? On the Mansfield Traquair website, buried deep in various hyperlinks, there is a 360-degree tour, but upon further inspection it needs Adobe Flash to function, which isn't available to all (like me). Although weddings inside this exclusive building are the reason for function, its access should be available to all. A woman-made mural from the late 19th century is rare and not allowing access from the general public is hiding important history and murals which revolutionised modern art in Scotland.

This amazing building is built near our school. I like the big red doors so much! I am still wondering if I can go inside the chapel. People said that the roof and windows are so beautiful. Everyday I go to school and I look at the top of the building, they look like birds flying. It has become a wedding venue. I think wedding people would like this place. You can search Mansfield Traquair and it will show you this building of art. If you ever get a chance to come and visit the chapel, you will love it. For sure! You can also call this building 'Edinburgh's Sistine Chapel', as it was its nickname. Even buildings love nicknames! There's a garden outside the chapel. You can have a look; beautiful flowers grow there. I loved the dandelions. And a tiny mushroom. It was cute. I visit every day when I go home after school.

In conclusion, this art should be free. This is an important piece of history, and it was a nice place to visit and should always be open for people.

15 Mansfield Place, Edinburgh, EH3 6BB

Calton Hill

Harlen R, Sophie W, Flo L

Calton Hill is situated in central Edinburgh and is 'mostly' famous for having a fire festival called Beltane.

Beltane comes from the Celtic word meaning 'fires of bel', a reference to the Celtic sun city, Belenus. The ancient Celts used Beltane to celebrate the coming of summer with fiestas and rituals that honoured fertility. Until the 19th century, the ancient practice of driving cattle between two rivers - a custom believed to magically shield the animals from disease - was still practised.

Some facts about Calton Hill include:
- Calton Hill is one of the first public parks in the country
- Nelson's monument was to commemorate Admiral Lord Nelson, who died at the battle of Trafalgar in 1805
- Nelson's monument was designed by architect Robert Burn not to be confused with the famous Scottish poet

- The National Monument of Scotland is a memorial to the Scottish soldiers and sailors who died fighting in the Napoleonic Wars. It was designed during 1823 by Charles Robert Cockrell and William Henry Playfair
- Construction started in 1826 and due to the lack of funds was left unfinished in 1829; it would have cost about £15,000 to £42,000. In today's money, £42,000 is equal to £4,432,842.11.

- Go to Calton Hill on a beautiful sunny day or go when the stars are out for a lovely view.

Dark History - The Witches of Edinburgh

Faye H, Crowley A

In the years between 1563 and 1736, many innocent women were tortured for being witches. The reasons needed to burn someone for being a witch were: no fingernails, blue spit, no toes, and the devil's mark, which can be anything from tattoos to moles to being poked with a needle and not bleeding. Most of these accusations can't actually be proven, because it's simply impossible for the body to have, so, a solution was created.

"Freezing liquid splashed into her face, travelling down her throat and up her nose. She inhaled, filling her lungs with the grubby water of the Nor Loch she was thrown into. She could see through the dirty water; she saw faces of disgust and happiness. From people she trusted and loved. Muffled screams were heard as the witch was ducked with bubbles bubbling up to the surface as she tried breathing, searching for oxygen. People watched as she looked around bundles of betrayal tumbling into her crystal green eyes.

"As they watched, she flapped around flailing her arms trying to come above the water to get a little bit of release from the burning feeling that was trapped in her lungs. As her legs kicked about, air got trapped in her flamboyant hoop skirt. She started to float up and she was kicking for another reason. She would rather die with her pride than die being called what she was not. A loud booming voice announced what everyone was waiting to hear. She floated and was sentenced to death by the fire of hell up on Calton Hill.

"As they chucked wood into a pile in an unsettling silence the woman was being dragged up Calton Hill, a gruff hand tightly gripping onto her frail arms. She kicked and punched with all her might but even a 'witch' couldn't break free from the hold they had on her. The smell of oil sunk into her senses as they roughly tied her to a pole with wood and lay at her feet. All she could think about as she looked at all the people around her was that they may be taking her pride, herself worth and her life, but she will not show them she is scared. Scared for herself, scared for her family and scared for the world that she lives in. She will go from this world with spite and belligerence. As they set her life up in flames she tugged and kicked and swore with great acrimony. A kick and a thrust she managed to get a burning piece of wood to fly at the crowd. Everyone flinched, some screamed, but all she could do was scream with laughter. Pain coursed through her, but she couldn't help but laugh at them as she was engulfed in flames and anguish."

If a person was accused of being a witch, they would be forced to go in the river. If she sank, she was innocent, however, if she floated, she would be a witch. They would be taken to Calton Hill to be burned.

A lot of women not only experienced being accused, but also experienced watching other women such as daughters, friends, mothers and other family be accused.

"Execution was something she always feared. She was shunned away from society because of what happened to her mother. Dragged into poverty by the grubby hands of law and society. Her mother floated as they dunked her into the river, her skirt collecting air. It wasn't fair. She had no word in it as she watched as they announced her mother was a witch; her mother was to be burned on Calton Hill. There was a tight grip around her waist as she screamed and pleaded for them to stop, they didn't even glance at her, she was a small mouse in a world full of cats and wolves, her voice may have been loud and overpowering but to them she was dirt on the shoe."

Witches for Scotland is a campaign for historic justice for the 3,837 people (mostly women) convicted and executed because of witchcraft. They are aiming to make Scotland address their barbarous past, apologies and add a national memorial to respect those wrongfully killed.

Section Two
Places of Interest

Forth 1

Abbey D, Rose A, Rifah R

Forth 1 is a popular, independent, local radio station that broadcasts to Edinburgh, The Lothians and Fife. Forth 1 is based on Forth Street, Edinburgh. Forth 1 has many different shows during the week such as Garry Spence, who does weekdays from 4pm and Saturday anthems from 6pm, and GBXperience by George Bowie, which contains party anthems and is open to requesting songs, on Fridays from 7pm. Then there's Boogie in the Morning with Boogie, Arlene and Marty from 6am on weekdays.

We interviewed Boogie from Boogie in the Morning.

Q - **Why did you want to become a radio presenter?**

A - I always loved music. I joined a youth club and one of my friends started a radio station, so I helped him and really enjoyed it.

Q - **How long have you been working at Forth 1?**

A - I have been working at radio stations for 24 years and Forth 1 for 19 out of those 24 years.

Q - **What makes Forth 1 better than other radio stations?**

A - Forth 1 is a local station so the news we talk about isn't just general.

Q - **What's your favourite part of working on the show?**

A - I really enjoy meeting different celebrities.

Q - **Who is your favourite person you've interviewed?**

A - Ed Sheeran and Robbie Williams since they are both super famous but still really relaxed.

Q - **How did Covid get in the way of your job?**

A - Immediately, I had to work from home. We're now back in the station but there's nowhere near as many people in the station as there used to be.

Q - **What types of events do you go to?**

A - I get invited to a lot of concerts and movie premieres. People tend to send you food from their local businesses so I can advertise it on the radio.

The Edinburgh Playhouse

Tahiyah R and Desi M

The Edinburgh playhouse is the second largest theatre in the UK, the owners are Ambassador Theatre Group. The capacity is 3059 people and it was built by John Fairweather in 1929.

The theatre opened on the 12th of August 1929 as a super cinema and was modelled on The Roxy theatre in New York. It was designed by the specialist cinema architect John Fairweather, most famous for his green's playhouse cinema in Glasgow.

The first play 1906 Cinderella. Now there are many genres and plays to watch to your liking, such as comedy, Disney and dramas.

These are our opinions on the Playhouse. We watched a show called Hairspray a while ago. It was amazing. If you're in Edinburgh, you definitely need to see it as it's a great experience.

We highly recommend going to watch a Disney show with your family or on your own. The experience is incredible and will surely be an amazing memory.

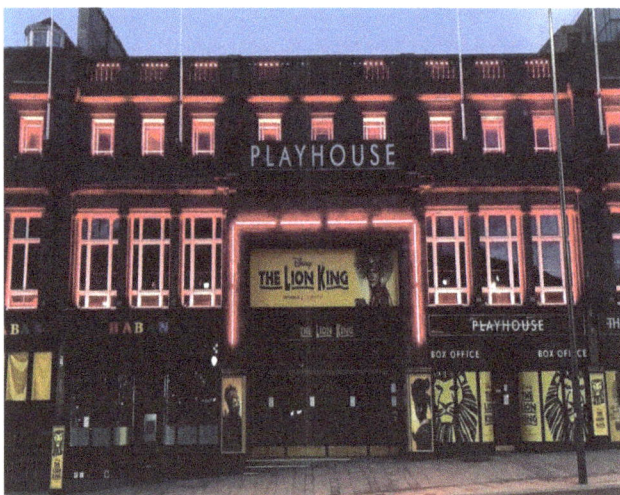

If you do decide to go the address is 18-22 Greenside Place, Edinburgh, EH1 3AA.

Section Three
Transport

Transport

Madi B, Miriam Q, Paris P

Welcome to the transport section, where we talk about the easiest, sustainable ways to get around the beautiful city of Edinburgh. This area covers all things transport so you know how to get around in a practical, sustainable way. Welcome to Edinburgh, we hope you enjoy your stay.

There are various ways you can travel around Edinburgh; you can walk, ride a bike, drive in a car, take a bus or even a tram. There are many different bus stops all around Edinburgh, so if you want accessible and affordable travel you could just hop on a bus.

There are many cycle paths across Edinburgh and lots of places to rent, borrow or buy bicycles. Cycling is a sustainable method of travel, and we are trying to promote it to prevent air pollution. At the time of writing this, tram lines are being built, so that's another way to travel. But if public transport just isn't your cup of tea, there are plenty of taxis and Ubers available.

If you don't have far to go, walking is the perfect method of transport. It is eco-friendly and completely free. There are also many wheelchair-friendly and guide-dog-friendly places to go around the area for those in need of extra support.

The sustainability aspect of getting around is more crucial than ever. With climate changes increasing at an alarming rate, it's key to know how to get around in a sustainable way.

- Bikes
- Electric cars
- Electric scooters
- Walking
- Skateboarding
- Carpooling

Bikes are a great way to get around with speed and having little to no carbon footprint.

Bike paths have increased in popularity over the years, making Edinburgh more useful to bike users.

With electric bikes/E-bikes being added into the mix, you can move even if you are tired. Bikes are a great way to soak up Edinburgh's history while enjoying the fresh air.

Buses have been around for over 100 years. Buses are a reliable way to get around the city. With the push for sustainable travel, Lothian Buses are making that push with their buses.

Carpooling is not the most sustainable method on this list. Carpooling is good because it allows multiple people to share a car, which cuts down on pollution.

Electric cars are an easy, quick way to get to your destination without causing great impact to the environment, compared to petrol/diesel cars. However, with the tram works causing congestion on the road, it can slow you down, so if you chose this as your method of travelling, be sure to leave plenty of time.

Electric scooters are a fast, easy way to travel around these busy streets. With bike paths usable, it is no wonder they have risen in popularity over the years. With a little carbon footprint, it makes it ideal to travel around the streets in style.

For transport there is a wide selection you can choose from like cars, buses, trams, etc. Personally, I prefer taxis and buses to get around Edinburgh. The most affordable transportation is probably buses because an adult ticket is £1.80 and for a child it's £0.90. Lothian Buses added a free bus card for people under 26, by using a Young Scot card, so it's easier to get to school. The bus stops are very easy to locate using Google Maps. Bus times are on an app called Lothian Buses. The app is very simple and easy to use. Although buses are public transport, it's comfy and the drivers are often very kind.

To get better at understanding how young people opt to get about, we interviewed 18 young people on their preferred methods. The most preferred was walking, with the bus coming two points behind. Car and bike were the least popular answers.

Section Four
What to do in 24 hours

What to do in 24 hours

Umamah B, Catrionah H, Holly B, Nabihah A

Broughton is a great place, full of great local shops and fun things to do. I hope you enjoy visits here and we'll start at the bottom of Rodney Street! You'll see The Marshmallow Lady first, a great local shop with some delicious products. Wander up the hill and feel free to find a bench in one of the small parks. If you go up past our school, and then the roundabout, you'll find lots of great local shops, but we would recommend The Chippy. Yes, it's called that, and it's on the left-hand side of the road as you go up towards the top of the hill. Head over the intersection and you will hopefully find Topping & Company, a little gem of a bookshop. On two floors, they specialise in signed copies. The itinerary ends at the top of Calton Hill, where you can admire the great day you've had.

Start your day with something sweet at The Marshmallow Lady. The Marshmallow Lady is completely different to other sweetie shops (candy, to any Americans out there). There are so many cool flavours like vanilla bean, After Eight, lemon souffle, Irn Bru, raspberry, cookies-and-cream, as well as many seasonal flavours like gingerbread or mini eggs. In the winter her hot chocolates are incredible and in the summer you can't beat her milkshakes. The shop is normally quieter in the mornings. Dogs are welcome in the shop and she sometimes brings her dog in! There are normally free samples for you to try, too.

After a trip to The Marshmallow Lady, there's more food in the cards. There is nothing better than some hot crispy chips with salt and sauce, an Edinburgh classic. The Chippy on Broughton Road has many other options beyond a typical chip shop, like gluten-free fish and chips, vegan options, and the 'sea dog'—a battered haddock in a hot dog roll. A tip for veggies: the chips are fried in beef dripping, so just ask for the vegetarian option and they will be happy to accommodate. You could eat your food in Bellevue Gardens behind the hedge over the road from Drummond High School, or in Barony Street park - down the lane of Barony Street.

Topping has to be my favourite bookshop. Its tall wooden bookshelves beaming with books and stories yet to be told. Spread over two floors, this shop has something for everyone and the staff will always help you find the perfect read. I love how there is always another hidden corner just for you. Two unique things about this shop are the tall ladders you can use to get to the highest shelves and the free tea offered around. This place is magical and anyone could spend hours here.

I chose Calton Hill because you have a 360-degree view of our beautiful city and it is not really much of a climb. Normally, I'll go up at least once a month because it has such glorious views. It takes around five to 10 minutes to climb. Pretty much anyone could climb it and if you're not able to you can drive your car up the hill, there's a road to drive up. There are also lots of nice places to sit and boards filled with information about the history and nature of the hill and the views of the surrounding area. The hill is filled with lots of greenery like bright yellow gorse bushes, green grass and luscious trees. The hill is exactly 100 metres high and the observatory up there is amazing. Also, Edinburgh's Disgrace is on the hill and is based on ancient Greek architecture, you can also climb on it. That brings up to the end of the day. Hope you enjoyed it.

Opening times and addresses:
The Chippy
Mon - Thur 4-9:30 p.m.. Fri and Sat 4-10:30 p.m., Sun 4-8:30 p.m.

79A Broughton Street, Edinburgh, EH1 3RJ
Observatory (Calton Hill)
Mon-Wed closed, Thur- Sun 10 a.m. - 4 p.m.
The Marshmallow Lady
Mon - Wed Closed, Thur - Sun 11 a.m. - 5 p.m.

14 Rodney Street, Edinburgh, EH7 4EA

£5 for a big bag of marshmallows
Topping & Company
Mon - Sun 9 a.m. - 9 p.m.

2 Blenheim Place, Edinburgh, EH7 5JH

Poem for what to do in 24 Hours

Broughton is the place to go
Great local shops and places on show
If you're looking for something sweet
Then this is the place to start
This is the perfect treat
It's a work of marshmallow art
Head to The Chippy
The local chip shop
The flavours are nippy
You won't want to stop
Topping is a great wee gem
The bookshop filled with magic
The old-school style will make you feel zen
Having to leave is always tragic
Up Calton Hill
The grass is green
It'll always fit the bill
The views are extreme

Section Five
Food

The Marshmallow Lady

Martin W L, Luca M, Kieran H F , Ali M, Michael A C

The Marshmallow Lady is a coffee shop that specialises in marshmallows. She offers hot drinks, homemade marshmallows, doughnuts and waffles.

The Marshmallow Lady is run by a lady called Nicole. Nicole makes marshmallows and has an enormous love for the confectionary, while also possessing a ludicrous commitment. Her craft of marshmallows is deemed as 'perfect'! Everything began in 2010 with a KitchenAid and no plan. She winged it and it worked. Everything has grown ever since. Her shop is beautifully decorated, and her marshmallows branch out in numerous varieties and flavours. Her shop is on 14 Rodney Street, Edinburgh, EH7 4EA. Shop hours are Mon - Thur, closed, Fri - Sun, 11-6. Her email is hello@themarshmallowlady.com and her phone number is (+44) 0131 629 7262.

Crombies

Martin W L, Luca M, Kieran H F , Ali M, Michael A C

Crombies is a well-known butcher near the bottom of Broughton Street. It's a butcher but does hot food, as well. The meat selection is large, including pork, beef, chicken, game, venison and other stuff.

I've known about Crombie's butcher and loved it for as long as I can remember. My dad has made and bought things that include the high-quality meat you get and everything I've tried hasn't had a single blemish to worry about.

The butchers first opened in 1955 when Alex Crombie opened the gates for his Broughton Street shop. The shop really got popular with the basic trading philosophy of providing "Quality, Value, Cleanliness and Service." He chose to trade slightly upmarket with good-quality meat, well-trimmed for its day with extra lean mince. His sausages were also very popular, supported with the slogan. Sadly, Alex passed at the age of 55.

Crombie's is very popular at Drummond because every day they do affordable lunches like toasties, pies, freshly cooked beef and chicken burgers, which I recommend. The service is always quick and the people working there are always happy to help. Definitely better than your usual fast-food chains! The quality is impeccable!

Opening times are Mon and Sun closed, Tue - Fri 08:00 - 17:30, Sat 07:30 - 17:00

Currently, Crombie's is undergoing a renovation! When it is done, they will do the classic meats, but also be a grocer selling more veg, fruit and other new wonders.

FED

Heather

FED sells smoothies, salads (with nice white cheese) and sandwiches with veggie options. At FED you can make your own sandwiches if you want, you can only make it with stuff they have. It has nice decor and a chilled vibe. There are lots of comfy chairs and sofas and lots of plants all over the place, making it smell like a greenhouse.

The health and safety measures at FED include masks during Covid restrictions and staff disinfect surfaces between visits.

When I visited with my mum and brothers we had the roto slice, the marz slice and chocolate shortbread. We all enjoyed ourselves.

2A Forth Street, Edinburgh EH1 3LD

Open Monday- Friday 7:30am - 3pm Dine in and Takeaway

Breakfast is served till 11am.

Down the Hatch

Rjay K

Down The Hatch is a Canadian restaurant which opened in December of 2020. They have two locations: 13 Antigua Street, Edinburgh, EH1 3NH and Port Edgar Marina, South Queensferry, EH30 9SQ. They serve a wide variety of food from burgers to wings to poutine, which is a Canadian delicacy.

From personal experience the food is great. I recommend the milkshakes and the burgers. The food is locally sourced, making it fresh and full of flavour. If you are passing by it is a must-try as the staff are really friendly and helpful.

It is also a one-of-a-kind restaurant in Scotland as the food is Canadian. The food is actually Canadian because the owner/founder is a Canadian who moved to Scotland years ago. He wanted to bring all the flavours to the Scottish palette. This is why Neil Davis opened his first restaurant in South Queensferry and named it Down the Hatch.

Kawaneko

Iona N

With this cafe's quirky cat-themed interior and delicious Japanese food, Kawaneko is the perfect place to have a nice lunch in the Broughton area.

Kawaneko is a restaurant/café located on Leith Walk. It is very affordable with food prices ranging from £5 to £11 and it has a wide variety of Japanese dishes which can be changed to suit the needs of those with allergies if needed.

Some examples of the foods they serve are: pork loin katsu curry, breaded pork loin with a Japanese curry sauce and rice, Japanese hamburger, steak, a rich beef and pork patty with Japanese gravy served with rice, cabbage slaw, braised carrots and a potato, and many more. You can also find some nice sweets such as chocolate brownies and green tea shortbread, along with many great drinks to mix and match your meal.

Open from Wed-Sat from 12pm - 8:30pm
Located: 62 Elm Row, Edinburgh, EH7 4AQ

Maki and Ramen

Carlos H

Maki and Ramen is a Japanese style restaurant and has 7 branches across Edinburgh.

One is located on Leith Street, another is near the Royal Mile and another is located in the St James Centre. The Opening times for the Leith Street Maki and Ramen are 12am - 10pm Monday to Sunday. The one near the Royal Mile is on Richmond Street, and it is open from 11.30am-3pm and then reopened 5pm-9.30pm. The restaurant in the St James centre has the same opening times as Richmond Street.

The menu includes ramen, sushi and more Japanese dishes. The food is exquisite and some of the design and decoration is just beautiful.

At Maki and Ramen they have loads of vegan and vegetarian options. The vegetarian option that I would recommend is the Pumpkin Katsu Curry. The vegan udon ramen is also a good choice.

Since 2014 Maki and Ramen have been giving Edinburgh amazing, tasty, fresh and healthy food with their handmade noodles and sushi.

The food that I recommend for everyone to enjoy is the Black Garlic Ramen. For a side dish, I would recommend getting the Gyozas, which are a type of dumpling. These are just my personal recommendations but there is so much more to choose from at Maki and Ramen.

Taste of Italy

Andres O, Dylan U, James P

I think Taste of Italy is an amazing place for family meals and special occasions or even a quick on the go coffee or ice cream. They even let you use the toilet if you are bursting walking past. They have fabulous food and the staff are polite as anything. Personally, I only go a few times a year with my family but every time I go I love it, apart from spicy pizza :(

Not too pricey

Opening times: 9am - 10pm

9 Baxters Place, Edinburgh, EH1 3EF

0131 557 9998

Shinsen Sushi

Vlad I

Shinsen sushi is a newly founded food outlet. Shinsen sushi specialises in sushi, teriyaki and overall just Japanese cuisine. Shinsen has quite an interesting story as even their opening was a risky move, as they opened during lockdown.

Originally Shinsen sushi was meant to be a pub. However, due to the lockdown the idea never saw the light of day. Luckily, they changed the idea to a sushi restaurant.

The food at Shinsen is frankly amazing. The rice is high quality, and the sushi is to die for and don't even get me started on the chefs themselves. The chefs are always kind to each other and to the customers and it is very easy to start a conversation with them. Personally, my favourite dish is the California roll. One of its many attractive features is the prices, for the quality of food it's quite the deal you'll be getting. Then again, I am biased as the owner of the restaurant is my family member, so if you want an unbiased view then go there for yourself and see just how good it is.

Location: 43 Broughton Street, Edinburgh, UK

Opening times: Monday - Saturday 12pm - 9pm, Sun 2pm - 9pm

Shinsen Sushi

Renee H

Shinsen Sushi is a small Japanese restaurant selling things such as curries, sushi, and rice bowls. There are also options for vegans and gluten-free. It's up Broughton Street and if you walk past you won't miss it :)

The menu (https://www.shinsen.co.uk/) includes foods such as soups, teriyaki, bento boxes and they also have sushi. My favourite thing I get there is the miso soup. It doesn't have too much in it and the packaging is easy enough to handle. The prices were also reasonable and wasn't too much to have.

When you take out it comes in a bag for you. The boxes, etc., are very compact and easy to carry, even if you didn't get a bag.

The decor is also very appealing and I enjoy looking at it. I haven't sat in before but it looks very comfortable, and when I see others inside they seem to enjoy it.

The pricing isn't too much and it is worth what you get. ££

Cafe Piccante

Martin W L, Luca M, Kieran H F , Ali M, Michael A C

Cafe Piccante is a fish-and-chip shop which offers an exquisite amount of food. Its speciality is deep-fried Mars bars, which are famous in the local area. It is widely considered one of the best fish 'n' chippy's in the area.

At Cafe Piccante we interviewed a former employee. She said that she was a waiter when she worked there. She served very friendly customers. Normally when she was working there, there were two other people working, too. There was one at the cashier and the other making food. Cafe Piccante has many deep-fried chocolate bars. Inside they have photos of customers that regularly go there. They sometimes have a disco night with customers. What she recommends is the fish dishes or the hamburger roll.

Cafe Piccante is up to standard, hygienic and enjoyable. It has nice and friendly people, regular people go there once or twice a week for a regular cup of coffee.

I like Cafe Piccante because the service is quick, the food is fresh, it's hygienic and it's for every type of person.

Some popular items: Fish and Chips, coffee, tea, juice, hamburger rolls for the morning.

I chose Cafe Piccante because it is just up the road from me, they serve things like breaded fish and chips surrounded by other shops. The fish is deep fried like the chips served with seasoning: salt, pepper, also with sauces like chippy sauce, ketchup, garlic sauce.

Opening times are Mon - Thur midday - 03:00, Saturday 15:00 - 03:00, Sunday 15:00 - 2:00

Fish and Chips

Liona H, Logan M, Lila G

There are four good fish and chip shops in the area.

- Cafe Piccante which is very good
- Giulianos
- The Chippy by Spencer
- Deep Sea, which is the best of these places, we think

The batter is the best part and try a deep-fried pizza, deep-fried Mars bar, donner calzone or burger.

You can get fish and chips delivered or go into the shop.

Greggs

Liona H, Logan M, Lila G

When you are in this area you need to go to Greggs. Things are £1 - £2. It is at the top of Broughton Street and on Elm Row. They do beautiful sausage rolls, very good doughnuts, great baguettes and pizzas. In the morning you can get a very good bacon and sausage sandwich. They sell soup, potato wedges and steak bakes. The best pie is a Scotch pie and the mince inside will melt in your mouth. Greggs is kind of a takeaway cafe. They also sell lots of good and cheap food. Also other snacks. The best things to get are a sausage roll and pizza. And yum-yums are good, as well.

21 Elm Row, Edinburgh, EH7 4AA
Mon - Sun 6:30 a.m. - 3:30 p.m.

Section Six
Shops

Typewronger

Yasmine E

Founded in 2017, Typewronger book shop is more than just your average bookshop. They are a community hub which shows off the best of our local area and local artists.

When thinking about what businesses I would like to write about, Typewronger instantly came to mind. From the moment you walk in the shop you are greeted with a cheery smile. The selection in the shop includes scribes (graphic art books done on typewriters), books and everything else in between. All made or written by local independent artists.

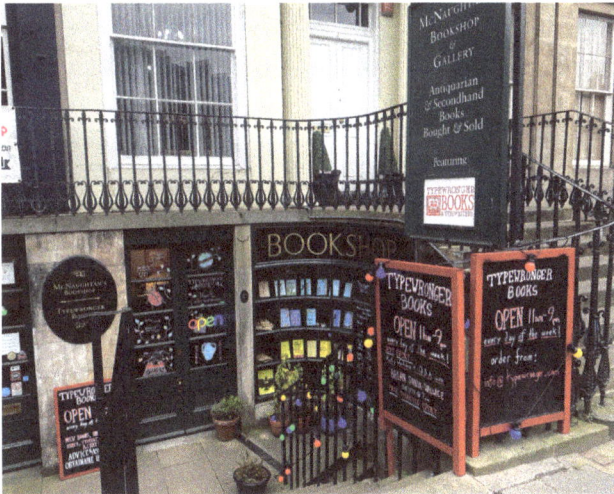

Luckily, I was able to interview the owner Tom Hodges. Here is a description of our conversation. Tom's responses to my questions show what a special place Typewronger is and how fortunate the Broughton area is to be the location for Tom's unique enterprise. Our conversation went a little like this:

I asked him who the most interesting clients are, and he said "I'm not sure if we can claim him as a client just yet but Tom Hanks famously wrote us a letter praising the shop! Hanks is a typewriter collector himself, and when we wrote to him to tell him about the new typewriter exhibition at NMA he wrote back!" I thought to myself how amazing this must have been. He then spoke about their press books, self published authors, and local artist's work. "It's a pleasure to deal directly with the people making these works of art and they offer us insights into their authorial intentions." Locals often praise this amazing shop and this is what Tom had to say about them: "We have a dedicated group of regulars who are always popping in for a browse and a chat. Typewronger is a talking shop so if folk just want to blether they stop on by! During the pandemic we kept up a free talking service through Zoom, Skype and the telephone so none of our regulars missed out on the chat." During the pandemic Typewronger stepped up to help their customers get through hard times by offering free Edinburgh wide delivery. They offered this service despite struggling themselves.

Tesco

Zuhaib A

Tesco is one of the most popular supermarkets in Britain with around 1000 regular customers every day. They treat their customers with utmost respect. They have good customer service because they acknowledge all of their customers and help them when they need it.

They open around 6am and close at 12pm but the most popular time is around 10pm.

They sell food, drinks and home goods, but it varies. Personally, I like Monster Munch because it has a nice crunch. Another good thing about Tesco is the fact that they try to limit their pollution by using electric lorries, by using energy saving lights in store and turning off fridges when they're not selling the alcohol in them.

If I had a choice, I would pick Tesco over other supermarkets because most of their products match what I need.

They have the best deals like the £3 meal deal!!

The Tesco I am talking about is the one at 7 Broughton Street, a perfect place to put a magnificent place such as Tesco.

Post office on top of Leith Walk

Andres O, Dylan U, James P

Post office is a corner shop located at the top of Leith Walk next to Greggs. It is a great little shop for food, sweets, drinks and if you are older it has the post office, vapes and alcoholic beverages for cheap prices. They have a wide range of staff with someone different at the counter everyday so don't bother trying to make pals with them.

20 Elm Row, Edinburgh, EH7 4AA

Mon - Sat 9am -5:30pm

Sunday - closed

Section Seven
Omni Centre

Omni Centre

Harris B, Jai H H, Seth O

The Omni Centre is an entertainment centre that includes many different facilities including gyms, restaurants and cinema. The Omni Centre was built in 2002 in Greenside Place with 10 floors, and on the bottom floor there is a car park with 990 spaces. It has the Edinburgh Playhouse beside it for entertainment, as well as the cinema.

The Omni Centre is an ambitious project built of glass. The signature metal giraffes were made by an artist who has sold their art even in Japan. These, interestingly, were made from scrap metal. These giraffes are called 'Dreaming Spires'

I, personally, like the Omni Centre. The best place included in the Omni centre is Cosmo. Cosmo is an all-you-can-eat buffet. It has loads of food from many different countries and you can eat as much as you like. Then, after you have finished with your main course you get dessert. The desert menu is the best thing there. There is a chocolate fountain that you can dip a multitude of things in. Cosmo is rated four stars and is a big all-you-can-eat restaurant. Cosmo is highly rated. 0131 524 7776. There are lots of other restaurants in the Omni Centre, these include: Nando's, Tony Macaroni, Cosmo's, Wetherspoons and the Slug and Lettuce.

The one thing the Omni Centre needs to fix is the prices of the snacks at the movies because they are WAY TOO EXPENSIVE. People just smuggle stuff into the movies because it's too expensive. But the movies are amazing and the latest Spiderman became one of the most-viewed movies in the world for a few weeks.

Omni gets the big hit movies.

It needs more recliners.

The movies are good, most of them.

There are two 3D movies, they are scary.

Opening times: Monday - Sunday open 6 a.m. - 1 a.m.
Info@omni_centre.co.uk
EH1 3AA
0131 524 7770
Address
Greenside Row

Omni Centre

Amanda N V O, Mia H, Olive E, James C, Gabriel A

We have chosen Cosmo because of their wide variety of food. Cosmo is a family-friendly buffet, entry price of £16 and after you may eat as much as your heart desires. Cosmo opened its doors in 2013 in Edinburgh, but was founded before, in 2003. Cosmo also tries to source locally, there is all sorts of food from around the world. There is a wide variety of food including delicacies from China, India, Malaysia, Italy and many others, with a range of dishes like teppanyaki, naan bread, and of course, pizza.

1. It has food from all around the world
2. It has really good customer service
3. £16 per person
4. It has a whole section just for desserts
5. Loud but nice environment
6. They have very nice workers and waiters
7. Great with friends

Giraffes of Omni Centre

As you walk past the Omni Centre you should notice the two very large giraffes standing grand. The majestic mother giraffe has the name Martha and the little one, Gilbert. These statues were opened to the public in 2002 and made of scrap metal from old bikes and motorcycles. The artist is named Helen Denerley. These beautiful sculptures reach a height of 22 feet for Martha, and the height of a smaller one I do not know.

Helen Denerley, born in 1956, is a Scottish sculptor. Her work is made from reused scrap metal and is inspired by the animal world. She has many sculptures around the world like Edinburgh, Hokkaido, Forres and Cromarty. She lives in Strathdon, Aberdeenshire.

The Playhouse

A commercial theatre, with plays for all ages, from comedies to dramas and even musicals. The interior is very classic, with a lot of royal design. The stage is very big and the seating area spreads out to three levels high, a lot of seating, leg space, comfy seating and lovely staff. During the plays there are breaks where you may leave the seating area, and go to the food and snack door, the prices are very good. The Playhouse is an old theatre that dates back to 12th August 1929; it's been kept in amazing condition for all of those years. I really like going there for a bit of fun and to have a feel of the classic interior and to relax from the outside world, to let yourself get pulled into a story. I have seen Beauty and The Beast and School of Rock as the musicals, and Hairspray, as well. I really recommend the musicals as they are very exciting and puts your frown upside down.

Restaurants in Omni

There are many restaurants in Omni. Tony Macaroni, which is an Italian restaurant that is open from 12 - 9 p.m., has a nice menu and drinks. Another restaurant in Omni is Nando's, its menu is mostly chicken and chips. They also have salad, sticky rice and mango, ice cream sundaes and pastries. There is also a Slug and Lettuce that has a lot of nice drinks like espresso martini, caipirinha and Aperol spritz. They have a lot of nice stuff to eat like burgers, wraps, lasagne and also have a nice amount of good desserts. Some are churros, ice cream and much more. After eating you can go get a drink at T'ea Tea. In T'ea Tea you can go get bubble tea and something called boba and you can get nice desserts. You can also get a nice view outside whilst eating your desserts. You can also get a nice view outside whilst having a drink. It opens at 12 p.m. and closes at 8:30 p.m.

Omni Centre

It is a great place for a cinema and to eat and have fun. The Omni Centre opened in 2002. In the Omni Centre there is T'ea, Nando's, Tony Macaroni, Cosmo, Wetherspoons and Slug and Lettuce. The Omni Centre has a lot of modern features like the windows. It has got a lot of great attractions around it.

Cosmo

Anna B L

Cosmo World Buffet is different from other places, as it has every food you would want to eat like pizza, sushi, chicken nuggets and French fries. It has desserts like popcorn, ice cream, marshmallows and pancakes. Oh, and pies and cakes, too.

They don't bring the food out to you. You get a plate and choose something you like. You can go up as many times as you like. The best food there is caramel apple pie. It is my favourite because it tastes sweet and delicious. Sometimes I go and only have that.

I go there with my mum, my dad and my brother. I go there for special occasions. I went there last time for my birthday on 6th June 2021. My family and friends celebrated my 13th birthday as Cosmo.

It's a very big restaurant and you have to book a table. I'm not sure if you can go in without a booking. I haven't been going there very long. I don't have a favourite time I have been there because every time has been AMAZING. It makes me feel joyful.

Section Eight
A weekend in Bellevue

Anna M and Farah H

We chose to do a weekend in Bellevue because there's quite a lot of places here and it's good to have a routine/direction from people that live/are used to the area so that you can enjoy your time.

On a Friday afternoon you can go to St James Quarter and do some shopping. There are a variety of different stores that you can go to for some lunch/coffee.

You can visit Erbil, a local takeaway, and if you spend a certain amount of money you can get two litres of Sprite for free. They offer a variety of foods, but our personal favourites are burgers, pizzas and slushies. Not to mention it's quite cheap. (Erbil is closed until 2023).

On Saturday morning, we recommend a local bakery called Soderberg. It's a Swedish cafe with seven branches. It's nice for a cup of coffee.

After your delicious breakfast, you can head over to Narcissus for some flowers for a special someone.

Afterwards you can go for a run to burn off the calories on the cycle path (which is traffic free).

After your run you can go and have a nice lunch at Eden's Kitchen. They have a nice stone stove. You can get cheap pizzas that are quite big. The staff are very cheerful, especially the cook. Or if you prefer a vegan alternative, a good fit is Harmonium.

A Saturday afternoon would be great spent in King George V Park, a great place if you have kids. There's a good slide, but you should sit on your jacket.

A Saturday evening could be well spent in the Michelin-starred restaurant, Fhior, where they have a 10-course menu package for £105, and if you want drinks to match it's £195.

On Sunday morning you can head over to the Bearded Baker for a nice morning breakfast. They offer coffee and baked goods.

After your nice breakfast you can take this time to explore the area, perhaps even buy a couple of groceries from the Tesco Express.

For lunch you can go into the amazing buffet Cosmos, which is located right next to the Omni Centre. After a tasty lunch you can have a convenient stop to the Omni entre and watch some great movies. To end off the day, you can head over to Nando's in the Omni Centre for a delicious dinner to end the day.

We hope this was helpful to guide you around Bellevue. Thanks for reading.

Section Nine
24 Hours in the Neighbourhood

Elliot I, Muhammad B, Ramzaan A, Emre G, Valentino O G

Introduction:

Hello, reader, welcome to our section of the book. Here, we won't just show you and recommend places you can go, but we will also show you a guide of places to go in 24 hours with a budget of £200.

24 hours

Breakfast 9:30

For breakfast we recommend a beautiful place called the Bearded Baker, which makes the most delicious cinnamon buns you will ever try, and it can be accompanied by a delicious cup of coffee to start the day.

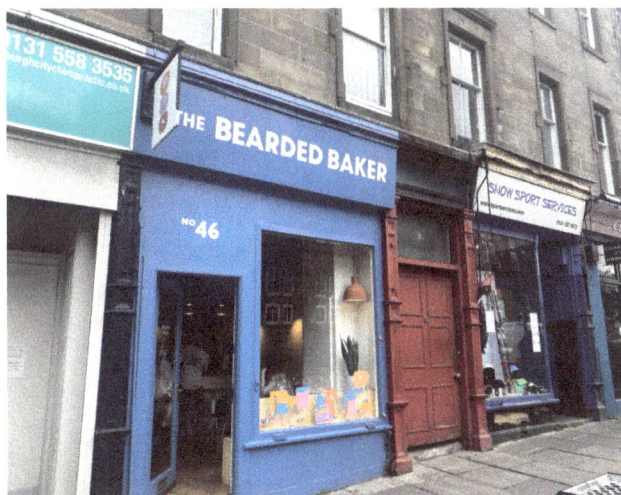

Walking 10:15

After your breakfast, we'd recommend to go on a 10- to15-minute walk to Edinburgh's newest shopping centre called St James Quarter.

Towards 10:30

Browse around shops.

Here is a list:

- Lego Store
- Bershka (anime tops)
- Bank of Scotland
- The Body Shop (soap)
- Bonnie & wild (restaurants and more)
- JD Sport
- H&M
- Hotel Chocolat
- And more

11:30

As a snack after all that wandering, you must be hungry. Go for a tasty snack at Krispy Kreme. Their doughnuts are top notch. So crispy, smooth and sweet.

12:30

After that delicious snack and a lot of walking around. At the top floor of the St James Quarter there is a bowling lane called Lane 7.

Lunchtime 14:00

After all that exercise you are sure to be hungry. Go to Wingstop for a meal you won't forget!

15:30 a lovely walk
16:00

Go to Omni Centre, and there is a Vue cinema. We recommend watching two movies and eat some more, of course, delicious snacks.

20:00 Dinner

Go to the amazing Jolly pizzeria and have the best pizza you will ever have, to round up the day.

   This is what we recommend doing. You don't have to do it this way. The budget we recommend is a minimum £200. This should cover it all. You can mix this up to your way.

Opening times and addresses:
Bearded Baker
9:30- 15:30
46 Rodney Street, Edinburgh, EH7 4DX
Estimate spend £10
Krispy Kreme
09:00 - 22:00
St James Quarter, Edinburgh, EH1 3AE
Estimate spend £15
Lane 7
11:00 - 00:00
St James Quarter, Edinburgh, EH1 3AE
Estimate spend £30

Wingstop
St James Quarter, Edinburgh, EH1 3AE
Estimate spend £20-30
Omni Centre
06:00 - 01:00
Greenside Row, Edinburgh, EH1 3AU
Jolly pizzeria
12:00 -22:00
9 Elm Row, Edinburgh, EH7 4AA
£30
Additional shops spend £56 - £100

Section Ten
St James Quarter

History of St James Centre

Aiden M

In 1964 the Burke Martin Partnership initially designed the St. James Centre but it was finished by Ian G. Cooke and Hugh Martin of Hugh Martin and Partners. The brutalist architecture of the government office atop the shopping centre made it one of the most unloved shopping centres in Edinburgh, but it was the busiest and most popular shopping location.

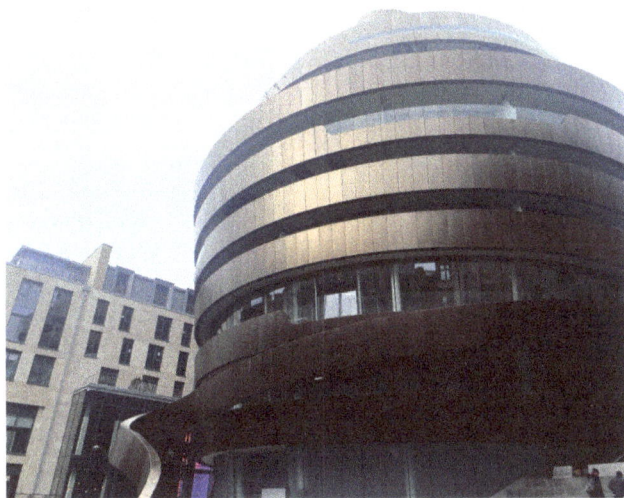

All of the shops in the shopping centre closed for redevelopment except for John Lewis. The old shopping centre finally closed in 2016 to be demolished. The old centre had over 60 stores, cafés and restaurants. In 2010 the old St. James Centre had many popular stores including River Island, Burton, Wallis, Next, Sports Direct, JD Sports, Subway, Game and Dorothy Perkins.

The new St James Quarter was designed by Allan Murray Architects BDP. There are over 80 shops, including the new Lego store, Sky and Samsung.

Leith Street

Opening times: Mon - Sat 9am - 8pm, Sun 10am - 6pm

St James Quarter

Kacey M, Jack T and Isla D

St James Quarter is a wonderful, sociable shopping centre with lots of shops, restaurants and helpful sources. One of the favourite helpful sources is the 'Dropit'. Dropit is a place where you can drop off your shopping if you've got lots of bags to carry; you can get them later or have them delivered to your home or hotel so you don't have to carry them around. If you are interested, you have to go to have a nosy. The St James Quarter's address is EH1 3AD.

There is a new bowling centre which is called Lane 7. It's located at the top of the St James Quarter and we highly recommend it. The Lane 7 has got glow-in-the-dark bowling lanes and food that you can enjoy after bowling or while bowling.

There is a new luxury hotel opening in winter 2022. It has 12 stories and has lovely stylish guest rooms. There is a pleasing spa which is located also in the hotel, great bar, 360-degree views. The hotel has a stunning rooftop, which will have a buzzing and aesthetic vibe, especially at night. The rooftop is also provided with a delightful bar.

St James Quarter opening times are Monday to Saturday 9:00 a.m. - 8:00 p.m. and Sunday 10:00 a.m. - 6:00 p.m.

Everyman Cinema is a new cinema opening early April 2022 with five screens, as well as a bar, restaurant and lounge.

JD

Alex S, Danyal S, Hamzah M, Nate T

JD Sports is a great sportswear shop that stocks and sells all the latest sports gear - from football kits to the highly coveted Nike Air Force 1s. As well as sports equipment. If it's sports-related you will be spoiled for choice as all your needs and wants will be catered for.

The new JD shop is located in the St James Quarter on the second floor of the all-new shopping centre.

JD Sports is one of the most popular shops that sells sports clothing and equipment in the UK and its range is enviable.

In our opinion, it is miles ahead of its main competitor, Sports Direct, that sells more dated and discounted merchandise.

In JD you can find the most popular brands like Nike, North Face, Adidas and Under Armour. But only the Glasgow football teams Celtic and Rangers are available to buy as football strips. Where are the Hearts and Hibs strips? A bit of an oversight on their part.

The most expensive item currently in JD Sports is the Nike VaporMax Plus trainers, which retail for £200. Although JD Sports are expensive, their clothes are really cool and fashionable and good quality. Nike is by far the most popular brand in JD Sports. In our opinion, it is the best shop in Edinburgh to buy trainers.

Also, the staff are really hot and helpful.

Opening Times
Mon- Wed and Fri-Sat 08:30 - 18:00
Thursday 08:30 - 20:00
Sunday 10:00 - 17:00

Address
St James Quarter
EH1 3AD

JD

Andres O, Dylan U, James P

JD Sports is a very popular shop located in the St James Quarter of Edinburgh. It has products by Nike, Adidas, Juicy, and many more. The shop specialises in women's and men's sport and streetwear. Personally I like JD Sports and, even though it's a bit pricey, it is worth the cost as it has great quality products. You could compare this shop to Foot Asylum.

Calvin Klein

Azzura M

Calvin Klein is an American fashion house established in 1968. They recently opened a shop in the St James Quarter. They sell pretty cool fashion and they don't have just clothes, they have fantastic perfume too and accessories like bags and jewellery. The perfume I like best is CK by Calvin Klein. The fashion is very popular as it is always very busy, although it is quite expensive. But, you can match it with anything you like. You can buy anything you want from Calvin Klein as it is a high-quality brand, it costs a lot but it is worth it. In Calvin Klein they have clothes for men and women. It is very popular with local people because the staff are very nice, the service is good and the products are attractive. I recommend a visit!

Lane7

Abbey D , Rose A, Rifah R

Lane7 is a family-friendly sort of entertainment in Edinburgh that offers a variety of activities under one roof for you to enjoy; bowling, digital arts, shooting pods, pool, arcade, shuffleboard and mini golf (coming soon) are among the different forms of entertainment available.

Lane7 also serves food. Burgers and fried chicken on various occasions have been quoted to be one of the best burgers.

It is advised that you book in advance, especially for bowling as it is very popular and always booked back-to-back.

Lane7's target market has been quoted to be "every single human being on the planet" and is highly recommended for everyone. It is available every day from 11am until late for you to enjoy the multiple activities with your friends and family. Overall, it's a really fascinating concept that we are sure you are going to enjoy.

It is an extremely unique place as there's nowhere like this in Edinburgh that offers so much stuff. You can find it on Floor 4, 02b St James Quarter, Edinburgh, EH1 3AD.

We interviewed the general manager, and he was very friendly and helpful. He told us that he loves working there, stating "there's nothing like it."

Lane 7

Jasmine B, Ruby F, Carly C

Lane 7 is a family-friendly bowling alley situated in the St James Quarter that offers lots of fun activities. Although Lane 7 is a bowling alley, it also offers darts, pool, ping pong, shooting pods, 'I Like Big Putts' crazy golf and shuffleboard. Lane 7 has five bowling lanes and you can have over 150 guests. Lane 7 also has food and drink, so you can eat while you play!

With a wide variety of foods from gluten-free and vegan options, there's something for everyone. They've got snacks, burgers, sides, desserts, pizzas and fries (loaded and plain). Don't forget the kids' menu!

Drinks-wise, for kids they do shakes, slushies, mocktails and soft drinks. For adults they do cocktails, wine and beer (bottled and draft). The prices for food and drink are fairly cheap for what you get.

Lane 7 is open daily from 11 a.m. to late. People of all ages are welcome, but under-14s must be accompanied by an adult and leave the premises by 10 p.m., at which point it becomes an adults-only venue. Lane 7 is in the all-new St James Quarter, the capital's most popular shopping destination. There are fantastic transport links and a huge car park on site. Directions to the bowling alley are clear and well sign posted. So you won't get lost! Lane 7 is a brilliant venue for nights out, parties and corporate events with karaoke, games and drinks. It even has karaoke. The atmosphere is vibrant and fun, you are absolutely guaranteed to have a great time.

Bonnie and Wild

Matthew D H

Bonnie and Wild is an amazing food court on the top floor of the St James Quarter that has stalls that make local Scottish seasonal dishes. Opened on 16th July 2021, there are currently eight concessions (two more upcoming) that provide various different dishes. Kale pizzas to fresh oysters, alcohols to grapefruit juice; the vastness of the menu will make you want to order everything! According to the manager, around 1,000 to 1,500 people visit in a day, so booking is recommended. The court is open from 9 a.m. until midnight.

St James Quarter (EH1 3AE) fourth floor. 0131 560 1800

No dogs unless they are guide dogs.

Churros, Baby

Layla O

The owners of Churros, Baby chose to open their business because the footfall is very high as it's near the St James Quarter. They opened on the same day as St James Quarter, which they said was very exciting.

Churros, Baby is a new kind of catering outlet based in a cool, colourful truck located in the St James Quarter. The owner describes how their business means that every day is different.

They had problems finding staff but apart from that they all enjoy working there because it's very vibrant and they never get bored.

They have had a lot of influencers pass but there's too many to name. The most popular toppings on their churros change every day. They said one day it could be Biscoff and the next day it's Nutella and marshmallows. They think if people see the other shoppers holding the churros, they start craving them and they want to buy them for themselves.

The Churros, Baby company are hoping to open in Glasgow one day. They weren't too badly affected by Covid as they are based outside.

I am a regular customer at Churros, Baby because not only do I love the taste of their products, I also find the people charming and helpful and their prices are very reasonable even for teenagers like me.

Section Eleven
Drummond Community High School

Drummond Community High School

Saif A

Drummond Community High School was made in 1925 by John Alexander Cafrae. The best thing about the school is the sense of community. One of the bad things about the school is the football goals; they are a little smaller than 7-a-side goals. Most of the teachers are friendly. If I could rate the school out of 5, I would give it a 4.

Wood F

My favourite place in the area is Cosmo. I like it because it has a lot of great food like prawns and sushi. You can also dip marshmallows into a chocolate fountain.

If I could add one thing to the area it would be more park places for the kids to play in.

Drummond Football Pitches

Ayomide O

They are there for people to enjoy at break and lunch times. We run around kicking the football and having lots of fun.

I use the football pitches every day at break and lunchtimes. I even use them in the rain. Football is my favourite sport. There are a lot of people who use them on a daily basis. They can be quite busy sometimes.

If you had never played football before you would need to know about offside, onside, penalties, free kicks and red and yellow cards.

Football Star

Ayomide O

Chapter 1:

There was a little boy called Tolu. When he was 13 he was happy because his dad David put Tolu in a football team named Liverpool from teens. He was good and became the world's greatest player in Liverpool for teens. Twenty years later he joined the real Liverpool. Tolu played very good. They named him the God of Football. A match was going on, Liverpool vs Man United. Tolu was about to score and a Man United fan flashed at his eye, almost making him go blind. The boy who almost made Tolu blind was fined $24,000.

Chapter 2: Tolu Interview

Tolu had an interview. He had a lot of nicknames like God of Football, and The Lion. Tolu said 'I was in love with football when I was 13 years old and I knew I was going to be a footballer' and the interviewer asked about the last game and he said 'No problem with that, it's just a jealous fan. My parents said I should be angry at a football match.' The interviewer was shocked.

Chapter 3: Tolu visits his old school

Tolu visited his old school Drummond High in Edinburgh. He had a great time at the school when he was younger. The school had an assembly one Friday morning. He met all the kids, who were surprised to see him at the assembly, beside Miss Zani, Mrs Barrocloth and Mrs Sloan. Tolu was there to give a talk on donating money to a kid who was interested in a football career. Tolu was giving money to the school for the development of a football team.

Chapter 4: Cup Finals

Liverpool was going to the Cup Finals. Liverpool versus Man United. It was a heated battle. Tolu was going with the ball. Twelfth minute he scored and it was 3-0 and Man United teamed up to injure Tolu but Tolu heard them and he told the ref. Tolu scored five more goals making the score 9-0. The Man United team tried everything to make Tolu angry but it didn't work so they gave up and 93 minutes in, Liverpool won. The head of the football managers made Tolu the captain of Liverpool.

Section Twelve
About the Authors

Sophie W

I learnt that Broughton has a strong community that has lots to learn about and explore.

I enjoyed spending time with the lovely, helpful.

I wished I hadn't missed a lesson!

Demi L

It was bad that H&M didn't answer our interview questions! It's alright though because we found a better shop. It was fun to work with the volunteers.

Danyal S, 13

My name is Danyal. I'm 13. I go to Drummond High School. It is in the city centre close to JD Sports.

Hamza M, 13

Hi, my name is Hamza. I am 13 and I go to Drummond in the Broughton area. I enjoy football and badminton.

Harlen R, 13

Harlen is 13 years old and lives in Edinburgh.

Ruby F, 13

I'm from Drummond Community High School and I like gymnastics, cats, reading, and TV shows. A TV show I've watched recently was called The Good Place, which is one of my favourites. I also own two cats called Matilda and Freddie who are eight and seven years old. When I'm older I'd like to go into law and help innocent people.

I worked well with my group and we were good at getting everything completed. I also did well at finding information for our section of our book. I worked well with the volunteers and teachers.

Jasmine B, 13

I'm a student at Drummond Community High School and I love to dance. I do ballet, commercial, contemporary, modern and acro. I recently did a competition and got a gold medal. I also like taekwondo and I'm hoping to get a black belt soon.

I think I worked well with my group and did well at completing the work. I really enjoyed working on the book with the volunteers.

Jai HH, 13

I exist the most.

I enjoyed the task and thought the volunteers were helpful and enthusiastic.

Harris B, 13

I exist, deal with it. Now excuse me I need to play my PS4. I like biscuits.

Demi L, 13

I'm Demi. I'm 13 and live in Abbeyhill and I go to Drummond and I like going out. I always make sure I look presentable, especially eyelashes. I would like to be an interior designer.

Evie U, 13

I'm Evie, I'm 13 and I go to school in Broughton, so I wrote a guidebook. I like being with friends. I always make sure I look good before going to school, especially makeup. I want to be a child psychologist when I leave school.

I've never done anything like this before but it was good working with a group of people of your choice.

Anna M, 13

Hi, I'm Anna, I'm 13 and my favourite things are NYC, fashion, Vogue and eyelash curlers. Something I want people to know is to buy Frank's Hot Sauce. I like staying home and watching Netflix. I like hanging out on Princes Street because they have Urban Outfitters, which is the best clothes shop.

Farah H, 13

Hi, my name is Farah and I'm 13 years old. I like music, food and video games.

I learnt how to interest people from all different cultures and backgrounds.

Fiona H, 13

Fiona likes art and drawing. She loves cats and all other animals such as insects. Fiona loves mushrooms and reading adventure books. Her favourite subject is all the subjects but she especially likes CDT and art. Her favourite place is the beach and she loves watermelon and chocolate. She wears (awesome) purple glasses. Fiona loves rainy and snowy days and she adores her family.

Jordyn B R, 14

Jordyn is a music lover and bookworm who is obsessed with crochet and cats. They are English but grew up in Scotland. They have gained the nickname Strawberry due to their red hair and green clothes. Jordyn is also a sucker for coming-of-age films and soppy romances but tends to read classics and contemporary fiction.

I enjoyed the project and all the nerves I had about taking it on just poofed away.

Theo T, 13

Theo loves music, he loves albums such as Whatever People Say I Am, That's What I'm Not (Arctic Monkeys) and How to be a Human (Glass Animals). He also loves shows, for example, Sherlock (BBC), Hannibal (NBC), and Good Omens. He also enjoys films from the '80s, '90s and 2000s, such as Heathers (1989) and Red Dragon (2002).

Madi B, 13

This is Madi, a school kid from Edinburgh. They enjoy reading and writing all sorts of things, especially poems and novels. They own two cats. They hope to get into a school in London in the future.

Miriam Q, 13

Miriam loves reading long novels and writing poetry. They also love listening to rock and jazz music while painting something abstract.

I enjoyed writing my bit on transport. I learnt how to write for an audience.

Paris P, 13

Paris is 13 years old. She likes playing Vibrant, Overwatch and Kirby Star Allies. And she likes reading manga.

Jack T, 13

My name is Jack, I'm 13 and I like making friends and I like playing basketball and golf. I also enjoy cooking.

Isla D, 13

Hi, my name is Isla. I am 13 years old. My favourite things to do include going to the beach, art, shopping, swimming, holidays, athletics and walking in the woodlands/hills. I also enjoy being out in the sunshine and I love summer time. I was born on 22nd July. I really hope you enjoy this book.

I thought that it was a great workshop and helped my literacy skills in many ways.

Michael A, 13

My name is Michael. I am 13. My birthday is on the 26th of December. I'm half Polish and half Albanian.

Ali M, 13

I'm 13, I'm sporty, I like cats and athletics. I go to Drummond High School and I went to Abbeyhill Primary School. My friends are Martin, Luca, Kieran and Michael. I go to outdoor sports activities like football, athletics and kickboxing. I like food and gaming. I also like drawing animals. My dad is from Asia, my mum is from England, and I was born in Scotland.

Martin W L, 13

My name is Martin. I like eating food and gaming. I go cycling and I like going on walks around town. I live near the school so I walk to school every day.

Luca M, 13

My name is Luca and I'm 14 in May, so close! I was born in and am Scottish. I'm also partially English and Lebanese. I love geeky stuff and video games, but most of all drawing. I've done drawing since I was young, like most people, and have kept doing it since. I like drawing everything and anything. Since I always wear shorts (because they're the best) that's my name in my English class! I don't mind it because some other names are much more strange.

Kieran F, 13

If you are reading this passage, I just want to say, why? To stop you from wasting any time you should stop reading this now because I have an average life, there is nothing special about me. All I do is go to school and then go home to watch anime and play games.

Elliot I, 13

My name is Elliot. I was born in Italy on 11th April. I used to do a sport called athletics. I was really good at it because I started when I was two. Sadly, I had to leave Italy when I was nine to come to this beautiful country called Scotland.

Muhammad B,14

My name is Muhammad and I am simultaneously 3.5 years old and 14, as I was born on a leap year. I enjoy writing and eating buns from the Bearded Baker (the cinnamon one, but the Lotus one is also very nice).

Valentino O G, 13

My name is Valentino and I am half-Italian and half-Spanish. I was born and raised in Spain. I came here two months ago, but I lived in England for one year.

I enjoyed it because it was a fun activity.

Ramzaan A, 13

My name is Ramzaan and I am 13 years old. I like to draw cartoon characters and I like Marvel.

Emre G, 13

My name is Emre, I am 13 and I like playing video games and sleeping. When I am at school I like to read.

Faye H, 13

Faye is an artistic and creative person who likes reading, writing and painting. She is a huge fan of The Twilight Saga and the Witches series (the books and the movies)

Crowley A, 14

A Criminal Minds addict who thinks Andrew Garfeild is the best Spiderman. They are also Faye's best friend and Faye is their favourite person in the world.

Carlos H,13

I like dogs, video games and parkour.

Iona N, 13

Iona is 13 years old. She moved to Edinburgh from America when she was 7 and has lived here ever since. She enjoys reading books and drawing in her free time. Some of her favourite subjects are geography, history and art. She prefers rainy weather as it is very ambient and the best weather to stare out the window and daydream while the rain streams down the glass.

James P, 13

My name is James. I'm 13 and I am in S2.

Andres O, 13

My name is Andres. I am 13 and I love football. I am from Edinburgh and I rep Btoon.

Dylan U, 14

Hi I'm Dylan, I am 14 in S2.

Layla O, 13

Layla is 13 years old. Her favourite subjects at school are Geography and English.

She loves watching South park, Fear Street and Superstore. She also likes listening to the songs 'Kissed by a Rose' by Seal, 'Material Girl' by Madonna, 'Cooler than me' by Mike Posner and 'Always forever' by The Cults. Her favourite authors are Stephen King and R.L Stine.

Yasmine E, 13

Yasmine is 13 years old. She was born in Edinburgh and is half Scottish, half Moroccan. One of her favourite bands is the Arctic monkeys. Her favourite subjects are modern studies, English and drama. Her favourite things to do are hang around with her friends and blast her favourite playlist.

Azzura M, 13

My name is Azzura M. I am 13 years old. I am from Italy. I moved to Edinburgh 2 years ago. My favourite subject at school is craft. In my free time I like to play video games like 'Call of Duty'. I like living in Edinburgh as I think it is a cool city but I am not so keen on the weather.

Rose A, 13

Rose is 13 years old and has lived in Edinburgh all her life. She enjoys playing instruments such as electric guitar and keyboard. As well as playing instruments she enjoys listening to music and has a very all over the place music taste. She also likes travelling and has been to places like New Zealand and Chile.

Abbey D, 13

Abbey is a 13 year old who loves to travel, in Scotland and all over the world. She has been to places like Morocco, Holland, Ben Nevis and Skye. She also loves music and plays guitar.

Rifah R, 13

Rifah is 13 years old and was born and raised in Scotland. She enjoys travelling and seeing different parts of the world with her family. A few of her favourite places she's visited include Turkey, Dubai, Abu Dhabi, Saudi Arabia, Italy and many more wonderful places. Somewhere she wishes to go next is Malaysia or Morocco. However, she would love to visit Dubai again as it was beyond beautiful.

Zahaib A, 13

My name is Zahaib and I am 13 years old. I am from Drummond Community High School and my favourite colour is green.

Saif A, 13

My name is Saif. I am 13 years old. I am in S2 and go to Drummond Community High School. My favourite things to do are to play football and playing my PS4. I don't like doing homework or any work.

Rjay K, 14

Hi, my name is Rjay. I'm 14 and I go to school at Drummond. I like a banter with my friends.

Tahiyah R, 13

Hi, my name is Tahiyah. I am 13 years old and I am Bengali. In my free time I enjoy going out with friends and going to new places.

Desi M, 13

Hey, I'm Desi and I'm 13. In my free time I enjoy going out with friends.

Vlad G, 13

I don't have anything interesting to write about myself.

Aiden M, 13

I like games.

Ana B L, 13

I like to draw Pingu. I have a brother; his name is Arthur and he is nine years old. I like to run. I like to play. I love my mum and dad and Timmy.

Liona H, 13

I'm 13 years old. I like going on my phone and going out with friends. And I like watching TV and my favourite food is probably Chinese or Indian. On TV I like to watch things like Euphoria and After Life. I also like to play the PlayStation. I like my cat, he's seven.

Lila G, 13

I like going on my phone. I like TikTok. I like my cat, he's two.

Mia H, 13

My name is Mia, I am 13 years old. I like music, singing, dancing and listening to music. I love sports and plants. My friends say I am good at art, that I have good fashion style and I'm kind.

Amanda N V O

#joinus #belieber4ever #OhMyGg #IAmWoman. My friends say I am artistic and a music lover.

Olive E, 13

My name is Olive, I'm 13 years old and lived in America for 12 years. I've been doing horse riding for eight years and have recently picked up archery at Lasswade Sports Centre. I love reading and listening to music. My friends say I'm nice, truthful and annoying.

James A C, 13

I'm James. I am 13 years old. I like going on walks with my friends for fresh air and talking to them.

Gabriel A, 13

Hi, I'm Gabriel. I am 13 and like animals and Marvel. My friends say I'm good at telling stories, funny, smart and active.

Ayomide O, 14

Ayomide is 14 years old. He loves playing football at school. His favourite subject is music and drama. His favourite word is amazing. His favourite thing is going to the beach at Portobello with his family for a walk.

I really enjoyed it, at first I didn't enjoy it as much as we were doing questions. Although now it's been so much fun. I had a great time doing my story about my love of football. And being able to write about it. I wrote 4 chapters and Miss Zani my PSA was ready to scribe more for my own book! It's been amazing and I can't wait to see the book published. Thank you

Catrionah H, 14

I love baking, cooking and loom knitting. Right now, I'm trying to learn French. I also really like going outside for walks, swimming and reading (in the past six months I've read 60 books). When I grow up I want to work in the social subjects area.

I liked working with Charlotte. Calton hill is pronounced 'Calton' not 'Colton'! I want to see the book in real bookshops.

Umama B, 13

I love cooking and crocheting. I speak two languages: English and Pashto. I enjoy reading books and listening to music. When I grow up I want to be a nursery teacher. Another thing about me is that I hate oranges and peas...but mostly oranges.

Holly B, 13

I've lived in Edinburgh my whole life. I live with my dog Blue. I really like crochet and travelling the world and one of my favourite subjects in CDT. I am learning French.

Renee H, 13

I like K-pop and my favourite group is Enhypen.

Class A

Class B

Class C

Class D

Acknowledgements

A huge thank you to Ms Tindall and Head Teacher Ms Robertson for welcoming us into Drummond Community High School to help create this second book. We are grateful for your partnership and your faith in our work. Every Tuesday from January through March had Sian, Claire, and I, as well as a team of very committed volunteers, made our way to some unconventional classrooms to work with the four S2 classes that wrote this book. Sceptical at first, the pupils sat down put pen to paper and created this guidebook celebrating the places and things they love about their school's neighbourhood.

Thank you to Sian Bevan who as the workshop leader for two of the classes helped to engage and encourage the pupils to take writing seriously and welcome the joy it can bring. Thanks also to our volunteers who came to work with the young writers. Many of the pupils may have started out as reluctant writers but your presence in the room, your hard work and your dedication was appreciated by each of them.

This book is one of the first in our new partnership with Calum's Legacy/Indie World Publishing. Calum's Legacy is opening up more opportunities for young people to have their voices heard through the publication of their own books. Their aim is to help kick start creative careers, providing work experience and employment for young people who want to develop their skills within book publishing and associated creative enterprises. They are a natural partner for the Superpower Agency and we are excited for what we can do together to support the creativity in young people.

The biggest of thanks to the young writers of this guidebook, the wonderful S2 pupils of Drummond Community High School. Look what you did! You wrote a book!

Volunteers

The volunteers of the Super Power Agency are integral to our projects. Our in-school programmes could not happen without their ideas, drive, and kindness. They help unleash our young people's most important super power: creativity!

We would like to extend the warmest of thanks to every volunteer who joined us on this project:

Classroom Volunteers
Aileen Brady
Jan Burney
Debbie Christie
Charlotte Cranston
Katie Dennison
Iain McMaster
Ellen Orrock
David Robinson

E.L.E.P.H.A.N.T volunteers
Anna Cooper
Marly Harper-Lalor
Stephanie Mlot
Courtney Smith

Thanks for the interviews
Craig at Lane 7
Manager in Bonnie and Wild
Lewis at JD Sports
Greg at Tesco
Boogie at Forth One
Andrew McCall at Maki and Ramen
Manager of Taste of Italy
Churrosbaby
Tom at Typewronger Books
Cosmo Edinburgh
Neal Davies at Down the Hatch

Lightning Source UK Ltd.
Milton Keynes UK
UKHW020832150622
404454UK00006B/173

9 781838 256838